Donkeys

Tessa Potter and Donna Bailey

STECK-VAUGHN
LIBRARY
A Division of Steck-Vaughn Company

This donkey lives on a farm but
does not work for the farmer.

2

The farmer has a tractor.
He does not need the donkey
to pull a cart.

The donkey lives in a field
with a horse.
The horse and the donkey are friends.

The horse only eats the good grass.
The donkey eats the grass and
all the weeds, too.
That makes the farmer happy.

The donkey rolls in the grass
when his back itches.
This is how he scratches his back!

6

The donkey belongs to Anna.
He is her pet donkey.

Anna visits her donkey every day.
She gives him carrots to eat.

Anna takes care of her donkey.
She brings him fresh water.

She puts the water in a tub
near the gate.

She makes sure the gate is closed.
Sometimes the donkey tries
to open the gate.

There is a shed in the field.
Anna puts fresh straw in the shed
for the donkey to lie on.

The donkey stays inside the shed when
it is very cold or wet.

Anna likes to ride her donkey.

First she ties the donkey to a post.

Then she puts on his saddle and bridle.

Now Anna can get on his back.
They ride around the field together.

Sometimes the donkey won't move.

When Anna pats his neck,

he walks again.

Anna and her donkey are good friends.

These donkeys are not pets.

They work for some farmers.

They pull heavy carts.

The farmers put vegetables on the carts.

The donkeys pull the carts to market.

Donkeys are very strong.

They can carry heavy loads.

This donkey has a big load of hay
on its back.

It carries the woman, too!

These donkeys are carrying
heavy loads of wood.
The farmers will burn the wood
on their cooking fires.

This boy is cutting sticks for firewood.
He puts the sticks in a basket
on the donkey's back.

Can you see the grapes in these baskets?
The donkeys are waiting for the farmers
to put the baskets onto their backs.

The farmers pick the grapes and
fill up the baskets.

The donkeys take the grapes
to the village.
The farmers will crush the grapes
to make wine.

These donkeys are carrying
baskets of salt.
The hot sun dried up the seawater and
left the salt on the ground.
The farmers put the salt in the baskets.

24

These people live in the desert, but
they do not stay in one place.
They use donkeys to carry their homes,
their children, and even their chickens!

These donkeys also carry people's homes.
Can you see the long poles
on the donkey's back?
The poles are part of the tents
the people live in.

When roads are too rocky for cars and
trucks, donkeys can carry goods
up the rocky paths.

This donkey carries tourists
up the steep track to the village
on top of the mountain.
He is called a "donkey taxi."

This donkey pulls a little cart to take
tourists around the city.

The donkeys in this city pull carts
filled with water.
They take the water to people's homes.

30

These people are filling up cans of
water from the river.
They need the water to grow their crops.

This man is watering his garden.
He gets the water from the bags
on the donkey's back.
The donkey works as hard as the man.

Index

Reading Consultant: Diana Bentley
Editorial Consultant: Donna Bailey
Supervising Editor: Kathleen Fitzgibbon

Illustrated by Gill Tomblin
Picture research by Suzanne Williams
Designed by Richard Garratt Design

Photographs
Cover: Survival Anglia
Frank Lane Picture Agency: 20 (Roger Tidman)
Peter Greenland: 1, 2, 6, 7, 8, 9, 10, 11, 14, 15 and 16
Robert Harding Picture Library: 17 (Michael Daniell), 18 (Michael Short),
    19 (Juniper Wood), 21 (S. H. & D. H. Cavanaugh), 24 and 28 (G. M. Wilkins),
    25, 26, 31 and 32 (Sassoon), 27 (Mani Kalash), 29 (Nedra Westwater)
NHPA: 3 (S. & O. Mathews)
ZEFA: 30

Note to the reader:
The donkeys illustrated on page 17 are from Cairo, page 18 - Crete, pages 19,
    26 and 27 - Pakistan, page 20 - Morocco, page 21 - Greece, page 24 -
    Cyprus, page 25 - Iran, pages 28 and 29 - Spain, page 30 - Saudi Arabia,
    and pages 31 and 32 - Ethiopia.

Library of Congress Cataloging-in-Publication Data: Potter, Tessa. Donkeys / Tessa Potter and Donna Bailey ; [illustrated
Gill Tomblin]. p. cm. — (Animal world) SUMMARY: Presents the life of a pet donkey on a farm and of donkeys who work as
beasts of burden. ISBN 0-8114-2631-9 1. Donkeys—Juvenile literature. [1. Donkeys.] I. Bailey, Donna. II. Tomblin, Gill, ill
Title. IV. Series: Animal world (Austin, Tex.) SF361.P68 1990 636.1′8—dc20 89-26079 CIP AC

1 2 3 4 5 6 7 8 9 LB 96 95 94 93 92 91 90